A SHORT EXPLANATION OF THE CLOUD THAT WILL MAKE YOU FEEL SMARTER

TECH FOR MATURE ADULTS

TODD HOFF

POSSIBILITY OUTPOST INC.

CONTENTS

1

STARTING OUR JOURNEY

"Todd, can you explain 'The Cloud'? What is it?" I was asked this question at lunch by Joe, a fellow tour member on a recent trip Linda (my wife) and I took to France.

It was not a question I was expecting on vacation, but with over 30 years experience as a programmer, a lot of it spent in cloud computing, it's a question I should have been able to knock out of the park. Except I didn't. My answer stank.

I hemmed and hawed. I stuttered and sputtered. I could tell that nothing I said was making any sense. I gave a horrible answer, and it has haunted me ever since.

While talking, I noticed a lot of other people at the table were interested in my answer as well. Many times during the trip Linda and I operated as a sort of unofficial tech support for some of the group. Our companions were all smart, accomplished people who'd achieved a lot in their lives. The thing is, they were just old enough that they didn't grow up with computers. Computers didn't come easily to them. They needed to be taught.

Kids these days understand computers because they're around computers all the time. They're what are called *digital natives*. A *digital native* is someone brought up during the age of digital technology, so they're familiar with computers and the internet from an early age.

It's like being a native speaker of a language. Someone born in France learns to speak French naturally, and they'll always sound more authentic and understand nuances of the language better than a student who took a few years of French in high school. If you aren't a native French speaker, you have to learn somehow. If you aren't a digital native, the same thing applies. You have to learn.

This book is the answer I wish I'd given Joe in France. It's short, to the point, and hopefully easy to understand. Here you go, Joe. I tried to do better this time.

2

WHAT DOES THE CLOUD LOOK LIKE?

Everyone talks about the cloud like it's some vague, abstract thing, when in fact it's a real material thing you can see and touch.

So before we get into the nitty gritty of defining what the *cloud* is, let's make the cloud real by taking a peek at what the cloud looks like:

Facebook

That's a strange image, isn't it? How is this a picture of the cloud everyone talks so much about?

What you're looking at is the interior of a *datacenter* owned by Facebook. A datacenter is just a giant warehouse-sized building containing lots and lots of computers.

How many computers? See those big glowy things in the picture? Each big glowy thing is called a *rack* and is about the size of a side-by-side refrigerator.

Notice how racks line both sides of the hallway, as far as the eye can see? Row after row of such hallways fill a datacenter.

Here's a closeup of what a rack looks like:

Facebook

Each rack holds dozens of pizza-box sized computers. If you do the math, the number of computers in a datacenter can range from tens of thousands to over a hundred thousand.

Now I can tell you a secret. The cloud is just a **big building with a lot of computers** inside. That's all the cloud is. Lots and lots of computers. Not such a big deal, is it?

So far we've only seen a Facebook datacenter, but a datacenter from Google, Amazon, or Microsoft will look similar.

Here's what the inside of a Google datacenter looks like:

Google

All those pipes are part of a cooling system for keeping Google's computers happy and healthy.

An Amazon datacenter looks a lot like a Facebook datacenter:

Amazon

We've seen what datacenters look like on the inside; let's take a gander at the outside.

Here's the outside of a Facebook datacenter:

Facebook

And here's the outside of a Microsoft datacenter:

Microsoft

Not that different than a Costco or Walmart, are they? But instead of selling quality brand-name merchandise, the cloud sells computers as a service. We'll talk a lot about what *selling computers as a service* means later.

When the cloud seems abstract and hard to understand, I want you to think back to these pictures.

At the simplest level, a cloud is just a big building full of computers. That's all it is. Nothing special is going on. There's no reason to feel intimidated.

See, you already know what the cloud is, and we just got started!

WHY IS IT CALLED A 'CLOUD' ANYWAY?

It's thought the term *cloud* comes from the symbol used to represent a network when drawing flowcharts and diagrams.

Why is it called a *cloud* in the first place? *Cloud* is such a strange name. It's one of those annoying words that doesn't give you any hint about what it means. It doesn't make sense.

How can a building full of computers be anything like the fluffy clouds we see in the sky?

The term *cloud* has a very practical origin. When engineers build stuff, they first draw a diagram of what they want to build.

On those diagrams, they use *symbols* to represent the different things they are building.

When building a house, for example, you use a symbol for a door instead of drawing a detailed picture of the exact door you want, knowing details like that will be figured out later (probably after quite a few arguments).

Wikimedia Commons

Let's say you are an engineer and you want to draw the diagram of a computer network that would end up looking something like this:

You can see all the computers connected by wires, all the tables, all the people; it's a mess! Would you really want to draw something like that? No way. No more than you would draw all the doors in a house plan. You would create a symbol to represent a network.

And that's exactly what the engineers did. The symbol engineers chose to represent a network was that of a *cloud*.

A cloud symbol on a diagram will always look something like:

Why a cloud?

Nobody knows for sure, but it's actually a brilliant choice.

Clouds are easy to draw. Clouds can be any size. So can networks. Clouds can have almost any shape. So can networks. We only see the outside of a cloud; what happens on the inside is hidden from view. We don't care how a network works. Clouds are made up of gazillions of tiny drops of water or ice crystals. Networks of made up of many pieces of equipment.

So it makes sense to represent a network as a cloud. They have a lot in common.

Using the cloud symbol, our new diagram looks a lot cleaner:

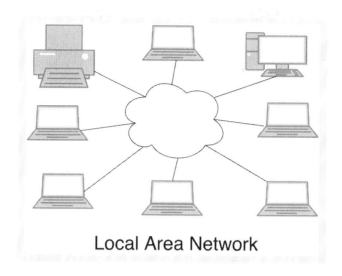

Local Area Network

It's simple and gets the point across, without all the messy real world details. Exactly what we want in a diagram.

The cloud symbol can represent *any network*; it doesn't matter what the network looks like or how it works.

What's a network?

A network connects things together.

A WiFi network connects computers to the internet. A highway system is a network of roads connecting places together. A cellular network is a network of equipment connecting phones together. A social network is a network connecting people together. A television network is a network of TV stations for showing program content. The IP Backbone Network is a network connecting all the devices that make up the internet.

These are all examples of networks. They are all very different in how they work and how they are built. Yet, we use the cloud symbol to represent all of them.

'The cloud' is short for cloud computing.

Remember our datacenter full of computers? It's just another network. All those computers connected together are made accessible over another network, the internet.

It was just a short jump from there to invent the term *cloud computing*. The term *cloud computing* was coined to mean accessing computer services over the internet.

That kind of makes sense, right?

In time, as cloud computing became a big business, cloud computing was shortened to just *the cloud*.

Whenever you hear *the cloud* now, it doesn't mean any network, it means a network of computers, accessed over the internet, that provides some sort of service. You don't care where those computers are located or how they work. You never see them. You never touch them. They are just a cloud of networked computers for you to use.

Let's Look at an Example Cloud Diagram

To see how the cloud symbol is used in real-life, here's a diagram of a complicated network:

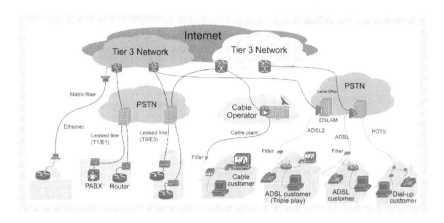

Wikimedia Commons

This diagram shows how various parts of the internet connect together. In fact, this is how your home internet connects to others on the internet.

Don't worry; it doesn't matter if you understand the whole diagram. Focus on the parts that look like clouds.

You should be able to see a bunch of different cloud symbols. There are two PSTN (public switched telephone network) clouds. There's a Cable Operator cloud. There are two Tier 3 Network clouds. A Tier 3 Network connects your home to the internet (think Comcast and Verizon). And there's one big internet cloud at the top connecting everything together.

This diagram is old. Since a lot of people connect to the internet these days using their cell phone, if it were drawn today, it would include a cloud for cellular networks.

Let's just look at one cloud, the PSTN. If you don't remember, ancient land line phones look something like:

A real diagram of the PSTN would contain a huge number of phones, an uncountable number of telephone poles, miles of cable, and an immense amount of electronic switching equipment.

It would be impossible to draw such a thing. Instead, we just draw a cloud symbol to represent the whole thing. We don't even bother trying to draw all the constituent parts.

We don't care how many phones or telephone poles are in the PSTN. All we care about is we dial a number, and we can talk to anyone in the world. How it works doesn't matter.

Same for the other networks in the diagram. The internet is hugely complicated. Don't care. All we care about is that we can connect to any other computer in the world over the internet.

Isn't that cloud symbol handy?

So now you know how that annoying phrase—*the cloud*—came to be.

Interested in more details? You might like Who Coined 'Cloud Computing'?

4

IF YOU USE ONLINE BANKING YOU ALREADY UNDERSTAND THE CLOUD

Now that we've developed an intuition for what the cloud looks like let's try to develop an intuitive feel for how the cloud works.

You've probably been using a cloud service for years; you've just never realized it. What is it? Your bank!

Banking has changed a great deal over recent years. To see how much, let me ask you a few questions.

How often do you go to the bank these days? Probably not as much as you used to. Standing in line to see the teller isn't much fun. How often do you write a check anymore? Again, probably not as much as you used to. Paying bills online is so easy. Do you know your bank teller's name? Probably not. Do you carry a lot of cash with you? Why when credit/debit cards are so convenient?

If you think banking has changed for you, imagine a time traveler from the 19th century, they wouldn't even recognize banking today. In their era a bank in a small town might look something like:

In those days depositing money in the bank literally meant placing your money in a small iron safe. Bank robbers loved those safes. They cracked like a thin shelled egg.

Remember all those old Wild West movies where bank robbers dramatically rode away with the town's money?

by Randy Franks

On the movie screen, Butch Cassidy robbing a bank is exciting, even romantic. In reality, that's your hard earned money they're stealing. As a kid I remember laughing as the townsfolk rustled up a posse, thinking there's no way a backwater sheriff along with a bunch of bankers, butchers, and bakers would ever catch our "heroes." As an adult, I now understand their urgency. Your life savings hung in the balance. If the outlaws make a clean get away, you're instantly penniless. Who wouldn't ride hard for justice?

Today, bank robberies don't scare depositors at all. Why? Technology has totally transformed both the nature of money and banking.

Money is Just a Number in a Computer

If Butch Cassidy were alive today, he wouldn't be a bank robber; he'd be a hacker because that's where the money is. Money today is just a number stored in a computer. And that changes everything.

Do you go into a bank anymore to check your bank balance? Of course not, that's so old school. Now you check your balance at an ATM, using an app on your phone, or from a website.

When checking your bank balance using an ATM, do you think a team of bank tellers runs back into the vault to count your fat stacks of cash?

Of course not. Nobody thinks that. Everyone knows their bank balance is just a number in a computer. The days of small iron safes are long gone. We intuitively know the computer always knows our bank balance and displaying it is as simple as asking a computer.

What else has changed? Think about what happens when paying for dinner with a debit card. You swipe your card. Swiping subtracts money from your bank account and adds it to the restaurant's account.

On the swipe of your card does our ready team of bank tellers rush into the vault and snatch stacks of cash off your pile and toss them onto the restaurant's cash pile?

Of course not. Numbers update in a computer. That's all that's happening. The number representing your bank balance decreases and the number representing the restaurant's bank account increases by the same amount.

Where does all this occur? Good question, I'm glad you asked. All the numbers are stored and **updated in the bank's cloud**. You knew we had to get back to the cloud eventually.

Remember what the cloud looks like? It's a big building full of computers. Your bank built a cloud, with lots and lots of computers. That's where your money is stored, as numbers, on their computers, in their cloud.

Checking Balances on an ATM — How does it Work?

You're at an ATM; you enter a valid PIN code. You press the "show me my bank balance" button. What happens next?

The ATM talks to the bank's cloud over an electronic communication network, which is a lot like the phone system, only it doesn't transmit your voice; it transmits your data.

When the ATM talks to the cloud, it requests your balance. That request is routed to one of the computers in the bank's cloud. The computer knows who you are because you inserted a card identifying yourself. The computer looks up your balance and returns it back to the ATM.

What language do computers use to talk? It's not so very different from words written in a letter. In fact, the whole process resembles an exchange of letters; only it's blisteringly fast because the exchange happens electronically.

The ATM sends a letter to the cloud, the cloud replies with a letter. Many letters are exchanged. Some letters are filled with requests; some are filled with information. A request looks like "send the bank balance for Joe." And an informational reply contains a number like Joe's bank account balance.

That back and forth style of exchange is how work gets done. Humans work the same way. We talk to each other. We ask each other questions. We ask each other to do things. Eventually, a task gets completed.

Of course, computers don't actually exchange letters. They exchange electronically transmitted packets of data, but the idea is the same.

Paying With a Debit Card — How does it Work?

The same process occurs when you pay for a meal with a debit card at a restaurant. You swipe your card on the card reader. The card reader talks to the cloud, letting it know who you are, which restaurant you're in, and how much the meal cost. A computer in the bank's cloud takes money out of your account and adds it to the restaurant's account. You're now free to leave the building.

What I just described, checking a bank balance and paying with a debit card, are services the bank provides. The bank implements both services using their *cloud,* so when you pay with a debit card or check your balance, those tasks are accomplished using a *cloud service.*

That's what a cloud service is, it's the things you can make a computer do for you.

If you're ever unclear about how the cloud and cloud services work, think back to this example. All these years when you've been using your bank, you've been using—unbeknownst to you—both a cloud and a cloud service.

So don't worry, you got this!

5

WHAT IS THE CLOUD?

Here's my definition of the cloud. You won't find it described like this anywhere else, but I think it will help make the cloud easier to understand:

The *cloud* is a *real physical place*—accessed over *the internet*—where a *service* is performed for you or where your *stuff* is *stored*. Your *stuff* is stored in the cloud, not on your device because the cloud is not on any device; the cloud lives in *datacenters*. A *program* running on your device accesses the cloud over the *internet*. The cloud is *infinite*, *accessible from anywhere*, at *any time*.

I'm going to explain each italicized word in the above paragraph. Each of those explanations may have more italicized words. I'll explain those too. I'll keep on explaining things until I get to a point where I don't think more explanation will help you understand any better. The idea is you can keep reading and rereading explanations until it all makes sense in your head.

Along with explanations, I'm going to use lots of examples. I'm going to explain in some detail how several real cloud services work. I'll also explain how services that aren't cloud-based work. Comparing the two approaches will reveal a lot about the cloud.

By explaining all the key terms and showing what they mean through examples, I hope the clouds will part, and all will become clear. That's the idea anyway.

Let's start by defining *real physical place*. This is easy. We already did it! In the chapter, *What Does the Cloud Look Like?*, we showed how a cloud is a bunch of computers that live in a gigantic building called a datacenter.

The cloud is real; it's physical, you can reach out and touch it; it even has a postal address. So the cloud is nothing to be afraid of.

If you do have a hard time understanding all these new concepts and ideas, don't worry, it's not you. This stuff is weird and hard to understand because it's so abstract. It deals with all sorts of intangible things like programs, data, services, and the internet.

I'll explain ideas in multiple ways, at times it may even seem like I'm repeating myself. At times it may even seem like I'm repeating myself, but I'm betting one of those approaches will help you make sense of things.

There are Really Two Kinds of Clouds: Cloud Providers and Cloud Services

I did such a bad job at answering Joe's question because, at the time, I didn't consider there were two kinds of clouds: *Cloud Providers* and *Cloud Services*. This gets confusing because in the news both will be called *the cloud* when they're two different things.

You will almost always use *cloud services*. Those are services running on a cloud. Remember how your bank offered services on their cloud? Apple's iCloud is a cloud service for keeping all your iOS devices in sync. It runs on Apple's cloud. Facebook Messenger is a cloud service for sending messages. It runs on Facebook's cloud.

As a programmer, I use *cloud providers*. Cloud providers own those datacenters we talked about earlier. Cloud providers let customers rent their computers to build services, just like you would go down to the local tool shed and rent a cement mixer, only the computers stay in the datacenter. They don't come home with you.

A cloud provider you may have heard of is Amazon Web Services (AWS). AWS is used by thousands of different companies to help deliver their services. You may have heard of some of them: Airbnb, BMW, Capital One, GE,

Netflix, Intuit, Johnson & Johnson, NASA, Nordstrom, and Yelp.

When I answered Joe's question, I gave him the *cloud provider* answer, not the *cloud service* answer. I didn't realize my mistake until much later. Let me explain. First, we'll need to talk about what a *service* is.

A Service is a Job You Hire Someone to do for You

The meaning of the word *service* seems obvious until you try to define it. Since we'll be using the word *service* a lot, it's important we have a good feel for what it means.

A service is **a job you hire someone to do for you.** You could hire help because it's a task you can't do for yourself, you just don't want to do, or you simply don't have time to do.

It doesn't matter why. The key is you hire another party to do a job for you, so you don't have to do it yourself.

We Use Services all the Time

We hire services all the time in real-life. In fact, about 80% of the US economy revolves around services. Services are everywhere.

If you, for example, don't want to clean your house, you hire a house cleaning service. If you don't want to wash your car, you take it to a car wash. If you don't want to do your taxes, you use a tax professional. If you have kids, you hire a baby-sitter. If your car breaks down, you hire a mechanic. If you're planning a wedding, you hire a wedding planner, who will hire a venue, a caterer, a florist, a band, a photographer and dozens of other costly services.

All the services we just talked about are examples of concrete services. You get something you can see, touch, feel, or experience in exchange for money.

There are other types of services that are less tangible. If you buy a cell phone, you need network connectivity, so you hire a company like Verizon or AT&T to provide network service.

Electricity is another intangible service. Your house needs electricity so you hire the power company to deliver it to you.

The cloud is more like an intangible service. We call services like water and power—utilities. In a way, a cloud provider creates a utility for computer services.

With that foundation, we can now understand the kind of services a cloud provider offers.

A Cloud Provider Rents Computers as a Service

A *cloud provider* is a company that owns a lot of computers and rents them out as a service. *Rent* means you pay good hard cash for using a cloud provider's computers.

Who are the major cloud providers?

The main cloud provider players today are Amazon AWS, Google Cloud Platform, and Microsoft Azure. There are many others, but these are the biggest and most popular.

For the most part, you don't have to care about cloud providers, no more than you care about who provides your electricity, water, or garbage service. You'll use a cloud service built on computers rented from a cloud provider; you will never have to deal with the cloud provider yourself.

What kind of services do cloud providers rent?

I'm going to list a lot of things that probably won't make sense to you, but here are some of the services a cloud provider can rent: compute, memory, storage, network bandwidth, caching, database, geographical diversity, disaster recovery, high availability, security, load balancing, authentication, search, machine learning, translation, image recognition, voice recognition, natural language parsing, DNS, payments, billing, queueing, notifications, email, and lots more.

Not every cloud provider offers all these services, but if you are a software developer, cloud services make your job a lot easier.

Why would anyone want to rent computers as a service?

For the same reason we use any service: we want all the benefits without all the work. All it costs is money!

The cloud provider is responsible for buying, maintaining, and operating their computers. All you have to do to use them is rent them. Everything else is taken care of for you. No muss, no fuss.

A Cloud Provider is Like a Car Rental Agency

Let's try a simple illustration. When you're traveling and you need a car, where do you go? A car rental agency. The car rental agency will always have cars for you to rent. That's the service a car rental agency provides. You don't own the cars. You don't have to buy the cars, store them, maintain them, repair them, or care about them at all. You rent a car when you need a car, and return it when done. That's **car rental as a service.**

A cloud provider is **computer rental as a service.** Just use a computer and return it when you're done. As with everything we're talking about, it's more complicated than that, but that's the basic idea.

A Cloud Service Performs a Job for you in a Cloud

We now know what a service is and we know what a cloud provider is. When we put them together, we get a *cloud service.* Imagine that!

What kind of job does a cloud service perform?

There are more cloud services than you can shake a stick at. Probably the most common job people hire a cloud service to do for them is file sharing and storage. A service like Dropbox, for example, offers a way to backup your data in their cloud and sync it onto all your devices.

To get a feel for how many services there are, here's a list with a description of the job each service performs:

• **Facebook Messenger** - exchange messages with people you know on Facebook.

• **Amazon** - buy most everything; sell and distribute products through their fulfillment system.

• **Apple iMessage** - exchange messages with with people you know who have Apple devices.

• **YouTube** - watch videos.

• **Google Maps** - figure out where you are and how to navigate to other locations.

• **Amazon Kindle** - read ebooks.

• **Gmail** - send and receive email.

• **Instagram** - share filtered selfies.

• **Twitter** - tell strangers what you had for breakfast.

• **Salesforce** - manage the relationship with customers.

• **iCloud** - sync data between Apple devices.

• **Google Apps** - a suite of group productivity programs.

• **Google Translate** - translate text from one language to another.

• **Box** - secure, share and edit all your files from anywhere.

• **DocuSign** - digitally sign documents.

• **Google Photos** - store and manage photos.

• **Evernote** - take and manage notes.

- **Facebook** - get annoyed by people you barely know.

- **Mailchimp** - create and manage email lists.

- **QuickBooks** - online accounting.

- **Spotify** - listen to music.

- **Pandora** - listen to music.

- **Netflix** - watch videos.

- **Yelp** - rate and review business and services.

- **PayPal** - send money and pay bills.

- **Uber** - get a ride.

- **Square** - accept credit card payments from customers.

- **Amazon Drive** - store files.

- **Microsoft OneDrive** - store files.

- **Carbonite** - backup files.

- **Adobe Creative Cloud** - Photoshop, After Effects, and other high-quality image editors.

This is an abbreviated list. There are many, many more services out there.

Most new services these days are cloud services.

Why? The cloud has many advantages over programs that run on only one device. We'll talk more about those advantages in chapters to come. Right now, let's take a deeper look at cloud services.

6

WHAT IS A CLOUD SERVICE? FACEBOOK MESSENGER AS AN EXAMPLE

What exactly does it mean when we say something is a cloud service?

It seems everyone is on Facebook these days, so let's use Facebook Messenger as our example of a cloud service.

If you're on Facebook you probably already know Facebook Messenger lets you send messages to other Facebook users.

Here's me sending a message using Messenger to Linda, my lovely wife and assistant for this trick, er, example:

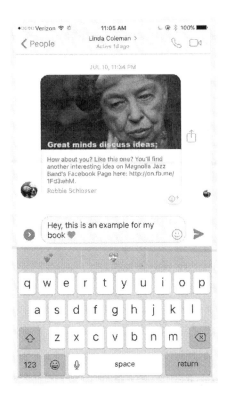

Even after all these years of using technology, it stills gives me a little thrill to know Linda received my message only a few seconds after I sent it, even though I was dozens of miles away when I pressed the send button.

On Linda's iPhone here's the message she received from me:

How did that message go from my phone to Linda's phone in the blink of an eye? You might have guessed the answer given the topic of this book: Facebook Messenger used the cloud to send my message to Linda.

A lot is going on here; let's unpack it.

First, we need to understand Facebook Messenger is a *program* or *app* that runs on a *device*. Let's quickly define each term. We'll go into more detail later.

A device is your smartphone, tablet, laptop, or desktop computer. It's any computer you happen to be using at the time.

The thing on the device that knows how to access the cloud is called an *app*. *App* is short for *application*. Facebook Messenger is an app. Tapping on the Facebook Messenger icon starts the app. You interact with the Messenger app to send and read messages.

Cloud services can also be accessed over the web, using a web browser like Chrome, Firefox, Internet Explorer, or Safari. In that case, you're using an app, the browser, to interact with a website over the internet. For our purposes, a website works like an app, so I'll treat websites and apps as the same throughout this book. Nothing changes.

In my example, the device I'm using is my iPhone. All my examples will use the iPhone, because, well, that's what I own. The app I'm using is Facebook Messenger. I downloaded Messenger, for free, over the internet, from Apple's App Store, on to my iPhone.

As you can see, the message I'm sending is "Hey, this is an example for my book." Great literature it's not.

When I tap the send button my message is sent to Linda. How? The cloud makes it happen.

Let's walk through how Messenger sends my message to Linda

- When I press send, the Messenger app takes my message, packages it up in an envelope, and sends it to Facebook's cloud over the internet, just like you would do when sending a letter. The package is called *data*. When you buy a data plan from Verizon or AT&T, this is the kind of data that counts against your data limit. There are separate chapters on both *data* and the *internet* later in the book.

- For now, you can think of data as both the letter and the envelope you mail using the postal service. You can think of the internet as a digital version of the highway the postal service uses to deliver letters. You can think of the name "Linda" as the address the letter is sent to. There's no stamp, so sending a message over Messenger doesn't cost you anything, which is why people like it so much!

- What does it mean to send my message to Facebook's cloud? It means my message is sent over the internet to one of the computers in one of Facebook's datacenters. Facebook has many datacenters around the world. Usually what happens is Messenger will pick the datacenter closest to you and send the message there.

- An app running on a computer in Facebook's datacenter reads the message, sees that I'm sending it to Linda, and puts the message in Linda's inbox. Facebook's inbox is just like the mailbox in which the postal carrier places your mail, except it's not physical, it's digital, it holds data, not letters.

- Linda also runs Messenger on her iPhone. The Messenger running on her phone (or any other device) will, over the internet, read her inbox in the cloud, see a new message is waiting, take it from the inbox, store it on her phone, and then display the message on her phone's screen for her to read. It's like you getting mail from the mailbox; only it happens using programs, data, and the internet instead of postal carriers, postal trucks, letters, and mailboxes.

So, that's what it means for a service to be performed in the cloud. Facebook's cloud was responsible for receiving the message, putting the message in the right inbox, and then handing over the message when requested. That's the basic service it performs. It may not sound like much, but in reality, the whole process is very complex. That's the idea though.

Once you develop an intuition for how Messenger sends messages, you understand almost every cloud service out there. They all work in a similar way.

Two Points I'd Like You to Notice

The cloud is a separate place.

The cloud is a remote place. It's not on your phone. The cloud doesn't exist on any device you use; it runs on computers in a datacenter. You access the cloud through a program you install on your device. That program knows how to talk to the cloud over the internet. This is why you can use a cloud service on any device. It's the program, like Facebook Messenger, that gives you access to the cloud, and that program can potentially run on any device.

Your stuff is in the cloud, not on your phone.

The cloud is always there. It never sleeps. Your stuff is always available in the cloud. My messages to Linda are stored in Facebook's cloud.

Let's say Linda loses her phone (which has been known to happen). When she gets a new phone and installs Facebook Messenger, she will still be able to see all her old messages. That's because her messages were not stored on her old phone. They were stored in Facebook's cloud, and Facebook has a humongous inbox that never gets full.

Facebook is their Own Cloud Provider

In my story, did you notice Facebook owns their computers and their datacenters? Facebook doesn't use one of the cloud providers we mentioned earlier; Facebook is their own cloud provider.

Why would a company want to own a cloud?

The biggest reasons are **money** and **control**. When a company gets really big, like Facebook, it's far cheaper for them to own their own datacenters. Economies of scale apply.

The other advantage of running your own cloud is you have complete control. That control means you can tailor every-thing to give your users the best possible experience.

Netflix, a service for watching movies and TV shows over the internet, is an example of a company that doesn't own datacenters. Netflix uses AWS as their cloud provider. Why? They don't want to manage datacenters. It takes a lot of time, money, and effort to manage a bunch of datacenters. Netflix decided they didn't want the hassle; they just want to concentrate on building their service.

Both Netflix and Facebook are massively successful, so either approach works.

7

WHAT ISN'T A CLOUD SERVICE?

I'll use my wife Linda in another example. I know she'll just love that. I can hear kvetching at me now as she reads this sentence.

Linda is an accountant and EA (Enrolled Agent, which means she's a tax expert). In her job, she uses QuickBooks, which is a small business accounting software program from Intuit.

For the longest time, Intuit only made a desktop computer version of QuickBooks. Now Intuit makes a cloud version called QuickBooks Online.

We're going to compare the two products as a way of understanding how big a difference there is between the two different approaches—cloud and desktop—of making and using software.

The Pain and Suffering of Using Desktop Computers

In case you haven't seen one in awhile, here's what an old desktop computer looks like:

Ah, the memories....

Software was sold in boxes!

How do you buy software for a desktop computer? It's quite the process.

First, you have to realize software used to come in boxes. Boxes? I know, right? How primitive.

If you haven't seen what a box of software looks like recently, here's a picture of the current desktop version of QuickBooks:

Linda uses a version of QuickBooks like this today, as do zillions of other accountants.

The desktop version of QuickBooks does have a nice looking interface. Here, take a look for yourself:

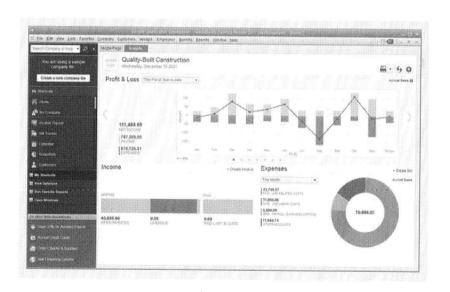

Nothing to complain about. It's state of the art. Buying boxed software is easy these days, but that wasn't always the case.

How did you buy box software in the olden days?

You had to drive across town to a retail store; browse shelves stuffed with awkward boxes of software packages; read the back matter on each box in a vain attempt to figure out what it does; finally pick a box off the shelf; take it to the checkout line and stand for ten minutes; pay with a check using your driver's license as ID; drive the box back to your office; install the software by inserting one floppy disk after another into a floppy drive, like an animal; pray it does what you want; scour the printed manuals to figure out how it works; wait on hold for hours as you call support to debug problem after problem.

I'm guessing kids these days have no idea what I'm even talking about. They've probably never even seen a floppy disk, or a VCR, or a video rental store, or film you have to get developed. Technology has changed so much over the years.

As horrible as all this sounds, and it was horrible, at the time **it was awesome.** A program like QuickBooks made your job as an accountant a hundred times easier, but let's **look at the limitations.**

QuickBooks was installed on a single computer that had to be purchased, maintained, and upgraded. Only one person could use it at a time. You had to be sitting in front of the computer to use it. All your precious accounting data was stored on the hard drive of that one computer. If that computer died, all your data was lost. If you were across town and needed a report, you were out of luck; the computer was back in your office. If you bought a new computer, you had to repeat the whole installation process and move the accounting data from your old computer to your new computer. And every year upgrading to a new version required repeating the same install process.

There's a lot of power in desktop software, but there are also a lot of limitations. How can we fix them?

Becoming a Cloud Service Changes Everything

Intuit built a cloud version of QuickBooks to solve the problems we just talked about; it's called QuickBooks Online.

Here's what QuickBooks Online looks like. Look closely... notice the difference between this version and the desktop version?

Did you notice the online version runs in the Chrome browser? At the top, you might be able to see the address bar containing Intuit's URL.

Yes, QuickBooks Online is a cloud service you use over the internet, as a website. That's what *online* means.

Many cloud services these days are websites instead of apps.

Why? Reduced development time and support costs.

Apps must be custom built for each type of device. The app

for the Apple iPhone isn't the same as the app for an Android phone, so it takes a lot of time and money to write both.

In contrast, once you make a website, it will work from any web browser. That means any device with a web browser can use a service, and that's very attractive to software developers.

Let's look at the benefits of QuickBooks being an online cloud service available over the web.

To buy QuickBooks Online, you don't have to go to the store. Just point your web browser at the website and sign up. Registering only takes a few minutes. No checkout line! And you don't pay with a check; you pay over the internet with a credit card.

There's nothing to install. QuickBooks Online is already installed in Intuit's cloud. No floppy disks! This is a huge advantage for people who aren't handy with computers or small businesses without an IT department.

You can use QuickBooks Online from any computer, from anywhere in the world. You do not have to be in the office to use it. This is important. There are times on vacation when Linda receives an emergency call from a client. If her client uses QuickBooks Online, then Linda can help them from France, or anywhere we happen to be, as long as we have a good internet connection. There's not much she can do to help if her client uses the desktop version.

Another advantage of an online cloud service is many people can use it at the same time. You have to pay for each user of course, but the restriction of one person having to be in front of one particular computer in the office is gone.

What's also gone is the risk of data loss if your computer dies. QuickBooks Online keeps your data safe.

You also don't have to worry about upgrading your software anymore. Intuit controls the software running in their cloud. They're responsible for performing any and all upgrades. You probably won't even notice when an upgrade happens.

There's no software to install or upgrade. Get a new computer, just log in to the website like normal. You can use any computer you want, from anywhere in the world, any time you want.

There are other less obvious advantages of having Quick-Books as a cloud service. One key advantage is an external accountant can just log in and see how things are going with the business. That's not possible using desktop software.

It's not all wine and roses.

An advantage desktop applications usually have is they are more powerful, meaning they have more features and functions than the online versions of the same software. It's often easier for programmers to make sophisticated desktop software, programming a website requires more compromises. That's just something to consider.

You'll need to use the desktop version if it has a specific must have feature. Linda still uses the desktop version of Quick-Books for this very reason.

8

WHAT DOES STUFF MEAN?

Let's remember the first line from our definition of the cloud:

The *cloud* is a *real physical place*—accessed over *the internet*—where a *service* is performed for you, or where your *stuff* is *stored*.

So far we've talked about the cloud living in datacenters as a *real physical space*. What we need to talk about now is *stuff*. Your stuff.

You know what stuff is in your house. Look around. It's filled with stuff like pictures, furniture, those dirty clothes that never quite make it into the laundry hamper. Yes, I can see those from here.

Hopefully, you don't have rooms filled with this much stuff:

Wikimedia Commons

You have lots of stuff on your phone and other devices too. Here are some examples: photos of trips you've taken, music you listen to, movies you watch, email you ignore, text messages you send, calendar events you make, spreadsheets you create, and the documents you write.

The generic name for all these kinds of *stuff* is *data*. *Data* is a record of stuff. We refer to anything an app understands how to *do something with*—as data.

We've already seen an example of what *do something with* data means in the Facebook Messenger chapter. If you recall, the data in that scenario was the message I sent to Linda. Facebook Messenger is the app that knew how to take my message and send it to the cloud so it could be delivered to Linda.

One way to think of data is like **ingredients in a recipe**. Each ingredient is a piece of data. It's the chef, or in our case, a program, that knows how to whip the data up into a delicious meal.

On the iPhone, the camera app is the app you use to take a picture. The **camera app knows** how to *do something with* pictures. Take a picture and the camera app stores it on your phone as data. Later, if you look at the picture in your camera roll, the camera app knows how to read the data from your phone and turn it back into a picture. Send a picture to a friend, and it's the picture represented as data that is sent. An app on their phone (or other device) knows how to turn the data back into a picture again. Data and apps always work together like that.

If you're a Star Trek fan, do you remember how the transporter works? An object is converted into an energy pattern and stored in a pattern buffer. The pattern is then beamed to a location and reconverted into matter.

Star Trek, sculpture by Devorah Sperber, Spock, Kirk and McCoy: Beaming-In (In-Between), Microsoft, Studio D, Redmond, Washington, USA

The **pattern is data.** The transporter is the program that knows what to do with the data. I hope, for Dr. McCoy's sake, all the atoms are arranged in the right order!

Here's a less futuristic example of what *do something with* data means. Let's say, as you receive receipts for purchases during the year, you toss them in a shoe box. At the end of the year, your accountant asks for your receipts, so you hand them the box. Your accountant cringes and gets to work turning those receipts into tax deductions. How?

Printed on every receipt is a company name, address, date, and dollar amount. Those are pieces of data, just like the message was in our Messenger example. Your accountant knows what to do with that data. Looking at the company name, for example, your accountant follows a set of rules to determine if a purchase is a business expense. That's the accountant's job, knowing what to do with all the data in your receipts.

Data can be used to represent any sort of stuff, like a movie, photo, a song, money, email, contracts, or even a hotel reservation. To a computer, stuff is all just data.

9

WHAT DOES STORED IN THE CLOUD MEAN?

Let's take another look at the first line in our cloud definition:

The *cloud* is a *real physical place*—accessed over *the internet*—where a *service* is performed for you, or where your *stuff* is *stored*.

We talked about stuff, but we haven't talked about what *stored* means yet, let's do that now.

When you have too much stuff in your house, you rent a storage unit and move all your extra stuff into it; that's what *stored* means. Your stuff is now stored in the storage unit:

In our Facebook Messenger example, we talked about how all of Linda's messages are stored in the cloud, not on her phone. You can think of the messages as *stuff*, or as we know now—*data*. You can think of the cloud as the storage unit. When using a cloud service, all your data is stored in the cloud.

Remember how we made the cloud real by showing what computers in a datacenter look like? Let's do that for storage.

Here's what cloud storage looks like:

Backblaze Storage Vault (Backblaze)

What are we looking at here? A storage vault from a cloud backup service called Backblaze. Each refrigerator sized cabinet is crammed full of *hard disks*. A hard disk stores and provides fast access to large amounts of data.

Here's what a hard disk looks like:

Wikimedia Commons

A hard disk is like a packing box in which you put small little bits of this and that. In your rented storage unit, you pile those boxes on top of one another as a high as they'll go. The more boxes, the more you can store.

That's the same idea Backblaze applies to their storage vault. Backblaze packs as many hard disks as possible into each cabinet, which is why it can store so many petabytes of data.

How large is a petabyte? Huge! Enough to store over 4,000 photos every day of your entire life. A datacenter will have racks and racks of these, almost too many to count.

Here's what similar disk storage unit looks like in Facebook's datacenter:

Facebook

So, just like how the cloud runs in a datacenter, your stuff is stored on real, physical, pieces of equipment. When you think of storing your photos, music, videos, and all your other data in the cloud, you can think of it being stored in something like the storage units pictured above.

The details change, but every cloud provider stores data in a similar way. There's nothing special about any of this. I hope that helps demystify things.

10

WHAT IS A DEVICE?

A device is your smartphone, tablet, laptop, or desktop

computer. These are just computers in different forms so we'll use device and computer interchangeably.

A device could be owned by you, or it could be supplied by your work, or maybe you're borrowing a device. A device is simply some form of computer you're using at any given time.

Devices come in many forms: iPhone, iPad, Android Tablet, Android Smartphone, Microsoft Surface, Dell Inspiron, Acer Aspire, or Google Chromebook.

They may all appear different, but for our purpose, they all work pretty much the same. They run an app that accesses the cloud over the internet. How they make that happen doesn't matter to us.

Let's use our Facebook Messenger example again. Imagine you wake up in the morning and use the Facebook Messenger app installed on your iPad to check if someone posted anything interesting during the night. Probably not, but it can happen. So, that's your first device of the day.

As you're sipping your morning beverage of choice, your phone chirps with an alert. A friend sent you a not very funny joke on Messenger, but their jokes are never very funny. That's your second device.

You get to work; your desktop computer has Messenger installed too. That's device number three.

Let's say you pick up an Android tablet or Google Chromebook at work and log into Facebook Messenger to check to see if you have any messages. Those are devices four and five.

During the day you could ping-pong back and forth between different devices but two things remain constant: Messenger and the cloud.

You're using the Messenger app (or web interface) on all your devices. And on every device, Messenger accesses the cloud to process and store your messages.

The key point is: it doesn't matter what device you're using as long as it has an *app* running on it that knows how to access the cloud.

11

WHAT IS A PROGRAM OR APP?

The thing on a computer that knows how to access the cloud is called a *program* or *app*. *App* is short for *application,* and an application is the same thing as a program. It's important to know both words—*app* and *program*—because they're interchangeable.

There many different examples of apps: Facebook Messenger, YouTube, Google Maps, Snapchat, Instagram, and Solitaire. Are you into games? If you play Candy Crush or Angry Birds, those are apps too.

On the iPhone, apps are downloaded from Apple's App Store. On an Android device, apps are downloaded from Google Play.

What is an app?

An app is a *series of instructions* telling a computer what to do.

Apps are what make our devices useful. Here's what the home screen of my iPad looks like:

Your phone, tablet, or laptop will likely look quite similar. It's full of apps! Each icon represents an app. Tapping any one of those icons starts the corresponding app. Starting an app causes the computer to read the app's program instructions, and the computer does whatever those instructions tell it to do. Tapping the Messenger icon, for example, starts Facebook Messenger. Once Messenger starts, you can begin sending and receiving messages.

What do program instructions look like?

They're a lot like the instructions you follow when cooking a recipe. Instead of being called a recipe, program instructions are called *source code*.

Here's an example of what source code looks like:

```
77 exports.timestamp = function() {
78    var str = "";
80    var currentTime = new Date()
81    var hours = currentTime.getHours()
82    var minutes = currentTime.getMinutes()
84    if (minutes < 10) {
85       minutes = "0" + minutes
86    }
87    str += hours + ":" + minutes;
88    if(hours > 11){
89       str += "PM"
90    } else {
91       str += "AM"
92    }
94    return str;
96 }
```

It won't make a lot of sense unless you're a programmer, but let's try to understand what a program does in general. Understanding the code itself isn't important.

Imagine explaining to a friend something you know how to do well and they don't know how to do at all. Let's use starting a car as an example. Instructions to start a car might look something like:

- find the car key
- find the car
- open the door
- sit down in the seat
- make sure the car is in park
- insert the key in the ignition
- turn the key
- confirm the engine has started

Look at the picture of the source code again. Each line is an instruction to the computer, just like each line in the car starting instructions is an instruction to a human.

The thing about instructions is that they can always be broken down into a lot more instructions. Just the *find the car key* step could be a dozen instructions.

The act of creating instructions with enough detail that the person you're instructing will be able to start the car is called *programming*. The text of the written instructions is called a *program*. Whoever creates the instructions is a *programmer*. The thing that knows how to interpret the program is a *computer*.

Computers understand far simpler instructions than we used in our *Start the Car* example, but the idea is exactly the same.

Not long ago it was humans, mainly women, sitting at desks, who performed the calculations computers execute today:

Shorpy

If you're interested, <u>Computing Power Used to Be Measured in 'Kilo-Girls'</u>, is a good read.

12

WHAT IS THE INTERNET?

Let's take a look at our cloud definition once again:

The *cloud* is a *real physical place*—accessed over *the internet*—where a *service* is performed for you, or where your *stuff* is *stored*.

At the start of our journey, to make the cloud real, I showed you a picture of computers in a datacenter. Unfortunately, that won't be possible with the internet. The internet is real, it is physical, but the internet is so many different things connected together it's impossible to represent with a single picture.

So, let's start simply. The word *internet* is short for *interconnection of networks*. The easiest way to understand what *interconnection of networks* means is to think of the highway system.

Here's a picture of the interstate highway system in the US:

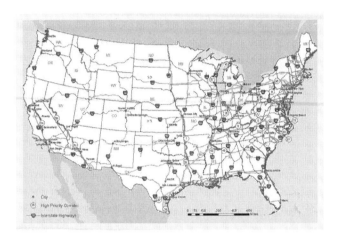

First, notice how the highway system is a network, where a network is a *group or system of interconnected people or things*. In this case, the things in the network are highways.

A highway is a long stretch of concrete, over which cars and trucks can travel, in both directions, at high speeds.

Looking at the map, it's clear that all those highways connect together. You can exit off one highway and get on another. In other words, the highways *interconnect*. It's because highways interconnect that you can plan a route from one side of the country to the other. In fact, many routes will take you coast-to-coast.

That's all an *interconnected network* means: there's a system of paths such that you can plan a route from one place to another over the network.

OK, now let's consider the internet. You can think of the internet as an electronic highway system for sending data from one computer to another computer. In other words, the internet allows computers to talk to each other.

The internet isn't made of concrete but from wires and cables strung across the globe. Electrical signals flow over all those wires and cables, carrying data from one place to another.

What does a map of the internet look like?

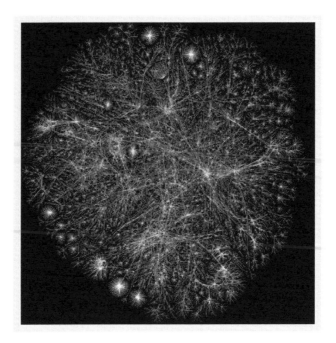

Opte Project

Beautiful, isn't it?

The lines in the picture are the wires and cables that form an interconnected network, just like the highway system. Data, sent over the internet, follows a route across the network to get from your device to the cloud service, and then back again to your device, just like you are taking a cross-country trip in a car.

How do you get on the Internet?

Every highway has an onramp, a way for you to get on the highway. What is the onramp for the internet? For your devices, it will either be Wi-Fi or the cellular network. At home, if you have a cable service, it's likely your cable company providing your internet onramp.

When you stop at a coffee shop and search for a Wi-Fi connection, what you're doing is stringing your own "invisible wire" from your device to the internet. Wi-Fi isn't a physical wire, it's more like a radio signal, but the idea is the same, Wi-Fi is a way for data to flow from your device onto the internet.

The cellular network is just another way to string an invisible wire from your device to the internet. When you buy cellular service from Verizon, AT&T, or any other cell provider, your device talks to a cell tower, using something like a radio signal. It's the cell tower that connects you to the internet. Data flows from your device to the cell tower, to the internet, and back again over invisible wires.

Some of the Cables that Make Up the Internet

There are a few things I can show you that might make this desciption of the internet more concrete.

Here's an ethernet cable. A lot of internet traffic flows over cables that look like this:

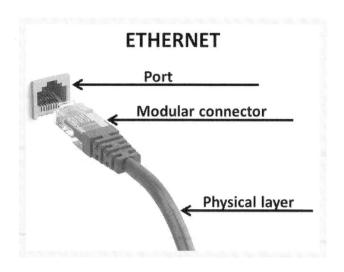

Wikimedia Commons

Have you ever wondered how the internet gets from the US to Europe? Or from the US to Japan? Those are some big oceans to cross. You might be surprised to learn giant cables run along the ocean floor, carrying the internet from one continent to another.

Here's what one of those cables looks like:

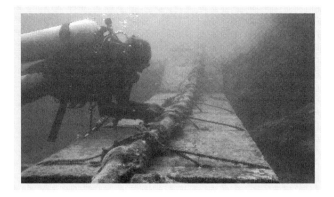

And here's a map of the many undersea cables carrying internet traffic across the world:

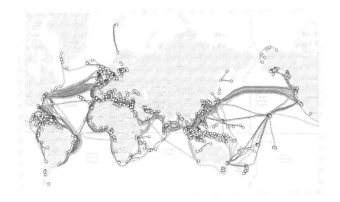

www.submarinecablemap.com

When I saw this map for the first time, I was shocked at how many under sea cables there were. Laying these cables must be immensely expensive. It seems people love their internet!

We talked about how your phone connects to the internet by first connecting to a cell tower. Here's what a cell tower looks like:

When your cell phone searches for a signal, it's looking for this kind of tower. Once connected, your data flows to the tower and then on to other parts of the network.

If you have a cable provider like Comcast, here's the type of cable connecting your house to the internet:

When you link all these kinds of cables together, along with many others kinds of cables and equipment, you create the internet.

13

WHAT IS A DATACENTER?

You were first introduced to the idea of a *datacenter* in chapter *What Does the Cloud Look Like?* I kept that chapter short and sweet because I didn't want to overwhelm you with information so early in the book. Here's, as they say, the rest of the story on datacenters.

What are datacenters for?

A datacenter is a building for housing computer systems and supporting components, such as networking and storage systems.

How many computers are in a datacenter?

It varies. A datacenter can have thousands, tens of thousands, or hundreds of thousands of computers.

Who builds datacenters?

Cloud providers. They build and own datacenters.

How much does a datacenter cost?

A lot. Modern datacenters can cost several billion dollars to build. Becoming a cloud provider requires deep pockets the size of the Marianas Trench, which is why there are so few of them.

Where are datacenters located?

Everywhere. A cloud provider can own one, a few, or dozens of datacenters located in every part of the world. The bigger a cloud provider is, the more datacenters they will have around the globe.

Why locate datacenters across the globe?

It's all about speed. The closer a datacenter is to users the faster computers in the datacenter can connect to users over the internet. That's why cloud providers build datacenters near large population centers. Faster internet connections make for a better user experience. Who likes to use a slow service?

A cloud provider like Google owns datacenters in around 17 different regions of the world. Accurate estimates are difficult to establish because Google is building new datacenters all the time, but this should give you some idea of their vast georgraphical coverage.

They have datacenters in California, Iowa, South Carolina,

Georgia, Oregon, Alabama, Tennessee, Oklahoma, Northern Virginia, Canada, Chile, Netherlands, São Paulo, London, Finland, Frankfurt, Mumbai, Taiwan, Singapore, Ireland, Belgium, and Sydney.

How many computers does a cloud provider have?

It's a secret. Really. They don't like to tell. Rumors suggest Google owns more than 2.5 million computers, but as I said, we don't know. What we do know is Google has oodles of computers, and they're buying more all the time.

14

THE GOOD, THE BAD AND THE UGLY OF CLOUD SERVICES

I've talked up the cloud quite a bit so far, but the cloud is not perfect. It has advantages and disadvantages. Let's take a look at some of them.

The Good

Cloud Storage is Safe

One benefit of storing stuff in a storage unit is that if your house burns down the stuff in the storage unit is safe.

The same is true for stuff stored in the cloud. Lose your phone, and your stuff still exists in the cloud. Get a new phone, and your stuff comes back. If your data existed only on your phone, that would not be possible; the data would be lost when the phone was lost.

Cloud Storage is Infinite

Cloud storage is effectively infinite. Your cloud provider adds new storage units all the time. While your device has a storage limit, the cloud does not. Of course, you do have to pay for it.

The Cloud is Available from Any Device at Anytime

We've talked about how this works a few times. Cloud storage and cloud services are accessible from any device at any time of the day or night.

Cloud Storage is Permanent

Storing stuff in the cloud has another advantage. It's permanent. It's stupendously hard to lose data in the cloud, but not impossible. Accidents do happen. Always make backups, even if your data is in the cloud.

A first class cloud service stores your data in at least three different geographical locations. If disaster strikes one datacenter, your data will still be available from one of their other datacenters. Remember how we said cloud providers had to have deep pockets? This is one reason why. It's very expensive to replicate data across all those datacenters, but as a result, your data isn't going anywhere.

There are two more common reasons why you may lose data: *you delete it*, or *you don't pay your bill*.

You delete it. Delete your data; it's gone. That's obvious enough.

You don't pay your bill. Most cloud services charge monthly or yearly fees. Stop paying your bill, or your credit card expires, the service goes away, and your data disappears.

The Cloud is Secure (Mostly)

There has always been a lot of FUD (fear, uncertainty, and doubt) thrown around saying cloud services are insecure. The question is always: insecure compared to what? Insecure compared to your home computer? Insecure compared to your office computer? Insecure compared to your laptop?

It's highly doubtful, unless you work for a company that takes security very, very seriously, that any of the computers you use will be as secure as computers rented from a top notch cloud provider. Google, Amazon, Microsoft, all employ armies of people constantly monitoring their cloud for security breaches. They're experts at security, and they have the time and money to do it right.

For example, AWS is PCI Level One Compliant, meaning the physical infrastructure has been audited and approved by an authorized, independent Qualified Security Assessor. All the top level clouds meet similar stringent security standards.

How about other clouds or other cloud services? That's less clear. Security is tremendously difficult and prohibitively expensive to do right. Software can always have bugs. People can always make mistakes. But unless you're the NSA or have special requirements, I wouldn't spend a lot of time worrying about if cloud services like Google Drive or QuickBooks Online are secure. They are.

When you get to second tier services, especially those that are free or very cheap, I would worry more. Always do your due diligence. Always do your research. Always ask a service to explain how it handles security. They should be able to tell you, and if not, stay away. But when it comes to top tier clouds and services, the odds are that they will be far more secure than anything you could build yourself.

Subscription Based Cloud Services are a Better Business Model

Programming, releasing, supporting, fixing and updating software is expensive. Paying once for a program is a lousy business model. It puts a lot of financial pressure on a business.

Users expect a company to support a program, provide bug fixes and add new features forever. There's just one problem: where does the money come from for all that work?

You've already paid for the program. No more money is coming from you. New sales can finance development costs for awhile, but sales eventually slow down. What then?

That's when businesses feel the pinch. Users will complain about a lack of bug fixes, a lack of new features, yet they'll scream bloody murder if they're charged for a new release.

It's a death spiral. A healthy business requires a constant stream of revenue to finance new development.

Since cloud services are almost always subscription based, they are assured of a predictable revenue stream. With that predictability they can hire people, buy equipment, rent facilities, build new features, improve performance, improve reliability, and they can commit to releasing updated software on a regular schedule.

Who likes paying monthly for a service? Nobody. But it works out best for everyone.

Cloud Apps Can Have Far More Powerful Features

We often think of desktop programs as more powerful than their app and web cousins. Features usually drop when a desktop program shrinks to fit inside an app or web interface. Everything is streamlined and simplified, often to the dismay of desktop users who miss the power of the old version.

What we're learning is **desktop programs are not always more powerful.** Cloud services can be significantly more powerful. Why? The resources available in the cloud dwarf the resources of any desktop computer.

Let's bring back our QuickBooks Online example, as, well, an example.

QuickBooks Online can automatically link bank and credit card accounts. With a single click, transactions import automatically into bank account registers.

Another improvement of the online version is you can create "Bank Rules" instructing QuickBooks how to categorize certain transactions. For instance, an electronic transfer of more than $600 that includes "Ford" in the description, can automatically be setup to be entered as a car lease payment. That saves a ton of work.

We're mobile beings these days. When you combine the ability of online services to be accessed from anywhere with the power of mobile computers like your phone, entire new capabilities open up. When you're on the road, for example, you can capture receipts using your phone's camera and upload them using QuickBooks mobile app. That's a feature you could never even dream of when using the desktop version.

There are still some areas where the desktop version is more appropriate, like job costing and inventory for certain manufacturing situations. But the online version is quickly improving. Before long, the online version will surpass the desktop version.

The Bad

Cloud Services Close Down

Want to know a dirty little secret? Yes, of course you do. Cloud services can disappear overnight.

Nirvanix was a cloud storage provider that went out of business with little or no notice. Sadly, many customers weren't able to transfer their data out in time. Megacloud was another online storage company that suddenly went bust. It can and does happen.

It's also possible for a service to close down because it was bought by another company. The buyer may choose to shut-down the service, or keep it going; it depends on their goals.

My favorite service in the whole world—FriendFeed—was bought by Facebook and brutally shutdown. It was a sad day. I still miss my old FriendFeed friends.

Regardless of why a service closes down, you might not have a chance to recover your data. All of it could be lost.

Cloud Storage Can Be Expensive

Usually, cloud storage has a low entry cost plan to get you hooked. Apple's iCloud, for example, gives you the first 5GB for free. Then, 50GB, at the time of this writing, is $.99 a month. That's $12 a year. 200 GB is $36 a year. 2TB is $120 a year.

Apple's prices are higher than most cloud storage providers. And 50GB may seem like a lot of storage, but keep in mind, every picture takes megabytes of storage. Recording videos at 4K resolution is a huge storage hog. And don't forget all the movies and music you keep downloading. Backing up your iPhone and iPad also takes up a lot of space.

Storage usage always increases. Each picture, each video, each song, requires more storage. The problem: storage isn't paid for just once. You pay for it, every year, basically forever.

Do you even need cloud storage? Not always. If you buy a 128GB iPhone, you can use that storage for free. You've already paid for it. Just keep taking pictures, at least until you run out of storage. And that's the problem. Data must be deleted to reclaim space. If you're using the cloud, all you have to do is buy more cloud storage.

The Cloud Can Be Slow

Let's say you want to view a photo. Which do you think will display faster, a photo stored on your device or a photo stored in the cloud? Depending on your network, it can be very slow to access the cloud over the internet. You've probably been in a place that had slow Wi-Fi. It's hell. In contrast, accessing a photo from your device is always consistently fast.

Usually accessing your stuff over the internet works just fine, but when it doesn't, it can be maddening. What a lot of programs do is store a local copy of your most recently used data on your device. It only goes to the cloud when there's a request for something not already on your device. Apple Photos works this way. Not every app does because it's hard to program correctly.

In the end, your cloud service is only as fast as your internet connection. If you plan to travel in locations with a slow or unavailable internet connection, then you may want to use an app that isn't based on a cloud service.

The Cloud Can be Unavailable

This is a variation of *The Cloud can Be Slow*. Sometimes the internet is not available. Maybe you can't find Wi-Fi, or maybe you have zero bars on your cell service, which means, your cloud services will not be available either. That's the advantage of using programs that work only on your device;

they work anywhere, it doesn't matter if you have an internet connection or not.

There are ways to work around the lack of an internet connection. Some apps can use the local device and then, when the internet comes back up, they'll sync whatever you did back to the cloud. Facebook Messenger will do this. You can send texts even when there's no cell connection, and when it comes back up, it will send your texts. Some apps, like Google Maps, can download a big area of the map to your device, so you can use it to navigate even when there's no internet connection. That's unusual though. And even Google only recently made this no internet connection version of Google maps.

The Ugly

It's Easy for Governments to Get Your Data

When your data is in the cloud, it's easy for law enforcement and the government to get your data without you even knowing it. All they need is a subpoena, and the cloud provider is required to give up your data. Just something to keep in mind.

Free Services May Sell Your Data

Running a cloud service is expensive. If you're not being charged for a service, you have to ask yourself, why? How are they paying for it? There are three potential answers to that question: *startups burning through cash, selling data for dollars,* and *using data for dollars.*

Startups burning through cash. One possibility is the cloud service is a startup trying to sign up as many users as possible, as fast as possible. They offer the service for free with the intention of charging for it later. This is the kind of service that can close down or get bought by a larger company, so be careful. Don't rely on this kind of service too heavily and make sure your data is backed up. If a startup goes out of business, they may sell your data as a way of making some money back for investors.

Selling data for dollars. Unroll.me is a service that helps keep your inbox clean by unsubscribing from email lists. A useful service for a lot of people. To know which email lists you have joined, they need to read all the email in your inbox. This should scare you right away. Letting anyone read your email is a potential security nightmare. But if you like the service, it may be worth it. What Unroll.me failed to clearly tell users is they were selling data from customer inboxes. Uber, for example, bought information on how many people were using Lyft. How did Unroll.me know this? They read your inbox. If you use Lyft, your inbox probably has a receipt from any transactions, so they just keep track.

AccuWeather, one of the most popular weather apps in Apple's app store, is another example of an app selling user data without explicit consent. AccuWeather sent geolocation data to a third-party firm to be used by advertisers, even when location sharing was switched off.

Using data for dollars. Google offers a massively popular free email service called Gmail. It's a great service.They don't sell your data to others, but they do use your data to show you targeted ads. That's how they keep Gmail "free." How do we know they don't sell your data? We don't really. We just "trust" Google. In this kind of arrangement you always have to ask yourself: do I trust them? Most of us trust Google...for now. Be glacially slow to trust an unknown service provider.

The rule is: If you're not paying for a service then beware. They have to make money somehow. One way to make money is to sell your data, which could be a huge violation of your privacy. Even if you are paying for a service, read their privacy statement to see what they are doing with your data. They can still sell your data, even if you are paying for the service. Move on if you don't like their privacy policy. There's always another service in the sea.

15

KINDLE: AMAZON'S CLOUD SERVICE
FOR READING EBOOKS

Are you already reading ebooks on Kindle? If so, this will be a great example of a cloud service for you. If not, let me take a quick detour and explain how ebooks work.

What are ebooks? They are electronic versions of a printed book that you read on a device. If you recall our discussion of data, an ebook is just a regular book turned into data. Once a book is turned into data then an app can read it on any device. If that doesn't make sense right now, hopefully, it will in a bit.

In 2007 Amazon introduced a device for reading ebooks called the Kindle. Here's a picture of one:

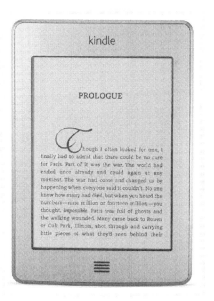

Amazon was not first to market with an ereader device like the Kindle, but they were able to transform ebooks into a big business. The secret sauce was Amazon's online bookstore.

Authors could upload an electronic version of their book into Amazon's book store; they didn't even need to create a paper version. Combine the ease of creating new books with Amazon's book selling expertise, and the self-publishing boom was born.

Now customers can search for a book, buy it, download it to their Kindle, and begin reading in a few minutes. Convenience won the day, and Amazon now leads in ebook sales.

Amazon also built a Kindle app for Apple and Android devices. Using the Kindle app, you don't need to buy a Kindle device to read ebooks from Amazon. Download the free Kindle app, and you can read almost any book you want.

Kindle is a Cloud Service

OK, we've described what Kindle is. Why do we care? Kindle is a cloud service. When you buy and download an ebook, the whole process uses a service running in Amazon's cloud.

Kindle is a perfect example of a cloud service because the Kindle app itself has two different views of the ebooks you've bought: a *cloud view* and a *device view*.

Cloud View

All the ebooks you've ever bought on Amazon are available in the cloud view.

Let's look at what the cloud view looks like in my Kindle app:

You know Kindle is in the cloud view because it tells you. I've conveniently circled the current view in yellow.

All the images are of book covers. Each cover is a book I've bought. Over the years I've bought hundreds of books, and I can look through all of them here. Remember, the cloud has infinite storage, so no matter how many books you buy, the cloud can handle it.

What can't handle storing all my books? My iPad. Storage is limited on my iPad. The solution is to download to my iPad only the books I'm reading right now. That's the device view.

Device View

Only ebooks you've downloaded to your device are available in the device view.

Here's what my device view looks like:

See, not many books are stored on my iPad, just the ones I'm currently reading. Tap a book cover in the device view, and you're instantly reading the book.

Downloading a book from the cloud is easy. In the cloud

view just tap on the cover picture and it downloads to your device. Switch over to the device view and the book will be there.

After I finish reading a book, I remove it from my device. Removing a book from your device doesn't delete the book forever. You still own it. You can always download the book again from the cloud view. Your books are always available from Amazon's cloud.

Why does Kindle go through all the effort of keeping a cloud and device view?

Two reasons: *limited device storage* and *reading without an internet connection.*

Limited device storage. The number of books you own can be far larger than the number of books that can fit on your device. You need a way of viewing all the books you've ever purchased, while also being able to read any book you want at any time.

Reading without an internet connection. Reading a book without an internet connection would be impossible if Kindle only had a cloud view. Remember, the cloud is only available over the internet. Nobody would like reading ebooks if they could only do it online. They might just stick to buying paper books instead of using Kindle.

I read books this way all the time. When I go to the beach, there's no internet connection, yet I can still read books on my iPad.

Cloud Services have More Cool Features

Kindle *remembers where you are in a book*. Let's say you're comfy in your living room reading a book on your iPad. You feel like going out, so you get a coffee at Starbucks, but you don't want to bring your big iPad.

Your book was just getting good, so while drinking coffee, you pull out your iPhone and start reading the same book from exactly the same spot you left off reading on your iPad, even though they are two completely different devices.

Kindle remembers where you are in each book. It stores your last reading position as data in the cloud. When you resume reading, Kindle asks the cloud for your last reading position. That's how it knows where you are.

As you're reading, you can highlight any passage from a book. When you read the book on a different device, Kindle will *remember which passages you highlighted*, so those passages will be highlighted on every device. How does that work? It's another cloud service.

You can also see the *most highlighted passages* in a book. If a lot of people highlight the same passage Kindle will notice and show it to you while you're reading. Yep, that's another cloud service.

Kindle also has a *notes feature*. You can write notes to yourself while reading. By now you know what I'm going to say: any notes you make on one device will be available on any other device you use to read the same book. How? If you said it's a cloud service, then you're right!

All these neat Kindle features—remembering where you are in a book, remembering highlighted passages, knowing the most highlighted passages, and remembering notes— would be impossible if a book only existed on a single device. There would be no way for all your devices to know about each other's existence to exchange data. But since Kindle is a cloud service, all these features are possible.

That's the power of the cloud.

16

ICLOUD: APPLE'S CLOUD SERVICE FOR SYNCING DATA

If you're an iPhone or an iPad user then the cloud you're probably most familiar with is Apple's iCloud.

According to Apple, iCloud: securely stores your photos, videos, documents, music, apps, and more — and keeps them updated across all your devices. So you always have access to what you want, wherever you want it.

Here's what my iCloud looks like over the web:

My experience is people have a hard time understanding what iCloud does, which makes sense, because iCloud is confusing. It works differently than the cloud services we've talked about so far. The reason this happens has to do with Apple's business model. Yes, their business model.

Apple's Business Model Dictates their Cloud Architecture

How does Apple make money? It sells hardware devices like the iPhone, iPad, MacBook, Watch and the iMac.

It's not hard to imagine Apple would like you to buy more of their phones, tablets, laptops, watches, and desktop computers. But ask yourself what would happen if all the services Apple offered were performed in the cloud and not on an Apple device?

Well, you wouldn't need an Apple device to use the service, would you? That means you wouldn't buy as much Apple hardware and Apple wouldn't make as much money. We can't have that, can we?

Apple Uses a Device Centric Model

Apple's approach to the cloud is different because *Apple uses a device centric model instead of a cloud centric model.* Apple wants the experience of using their devices to be seamless and consistent. They don't want data compartmentalized on each device.

Add a contact on your iPhone and Apple wants that contact to be on your iPad the next time you use it. If that contact weren't on your iPad, you'd be angry, which isn't the kind of experience Apple wants you to have.

Apple makes all your devices work together by syncing data between them. *Sync* means keep synchronized, meaning a change on one device is reflected on all your other devices. Delete a contact on one device, and it's deleted everywhere. Add a contact, and it's added everywhere.

iCloud is the cloud service doing all this behind the scenes syncing. iCloud combines the power of all the computers in Apple's cloud with programs running on each of your devices. Together they keep all your Apple devices synchronized with each other.

What kind of data does Apple sync between your devices?

Photos, Contacts, Mail, Calendars, Reminders, Pages, Numbers, Notes, Safari, News, and much more. iCloud constantly syncs all these different kinds of data between your devices.

As an example, if you have iCloud turned on and you take a photo on your phone, iCloud will sync that photo to all your devices. Look at your photo library on your iPad. The picture you took on your phone shows up there, soon after you took it.

All your photos (and other data) are securely stored in Apple's cloud. Even if you lose all your devices, you won't lose your photos. Apple tucks them safely away in their cloud. Get a new phone, log into your Apple account, and all your photos will magically appear.

Storing all your photos in the cloud lets Apple play a clever trick: you can take more photos than will fit on any of your devices (as long as you've paid for the cloud storage). How? Apple stores on each device the photos it thinks you are most likely to view. This will be different for each device because each device has different amounts of available storage. All your other photos are still up in the cloud. When you want to see a photo that's not on the device, Apple copies it to your device and removes some other photo to make room.

Comparing Apple to Google

Since Google is a major alternative to iCloud, it will help to understand how they differ. Google usually does not sync data between devices (though it can). Google Photos, which is Google's cloud service for managing photos, has every device access your photos directly from their cloud. No syncing needed. This is one reason why Google can make a version of their apps available on iOS, Android, and the web, while Apple apps work primarily on Apple devices.

Apple vs. Google Pros and Cons

How iCloud works is not wrong, or bad. It's just different and quite clever. However, there are pros and cons to Apple's cloud strategy.

The biggest con is getting the syncing right is extraordinarily complex, like rocket-science complex. In practice, this means there can be bugs in how the syncing works. Your data will be on one device and not on another, and you'll have no idea why or what to do about it.

The biggest pro is your data is available on your device. All your data is there, even without an internet connection, and accessing that data will be fast.

Should you use iCloud?

Once upon a time I would have said no. iCloud used to be buggy. It had lots of problems with data not syncing properly. Apple has ironed out most of those problems, so it's reliable enough to use now.

If you primarily use Apple devices, then iCloud is almost a no brainer. Yes, it's more expensive than it should be, but iCloud makes syncing painless so it's worth the cost. And if your family primarily uses Apple devices, it's a double no brainer, because there are a lot of cool features that allow families to share data with each other.

A huge downside of iCloud is that it only works on Apple devices. That's not completely true; some of the iCloud works on Windows, and over the web, but I wouldn't trust Apple's commitment to any non-Apple platform. Apple really wants to keep you in their ecosystem. Support for other platforms is likely to fall low on the priority list when it comes to fixing bugs and adding features.

If you use a mix of platforms, like Windows and Android, then iCloud may not be for you. You'll probably want to choose Google or a service from another vendor. A lot of people happily use Dropbox to sync files between all their devices, including Android and Windows devices. Dropbox, however, can't sync settings, photos, notes, contacts, and other data between iOS devices; only Apple can do that.

A huge advantage of iCloud is that it makes it easy to backup your iOS devices. We've talked about the importance of backing up your data many times. iCloud is how you do it. However, iCloud won't backup a laptop or desktop computer for you; you'll need to use another service like Carbonite.

You may find yourself using a mix of different services for different jobs. Use iCloud for your Apple devices. If you collaborate on documents with a group, Google Drive is often the way to go. And if you need to sync files between many kinds of different devices and share them with other people, then Dropbox is a popular option.

17

GOOGLE MAPS: A CLOUD SERVICE FOR NAVIGATION

I'm horrible with directions. So for me, the biggest use for my phone, is turn-by-turn navigation. It's a godsend. In fact, I programmed an iPhone app, called PicBak, to help me with directions.

Which app do I use for navigation? Google Maps. Apple Maps used to be horrible, and even though it's pretty good now, my default is good old trusty Google Maps. I have confidence Google Maps will always get me where I'm going.

Here's what Google Maps looks like:

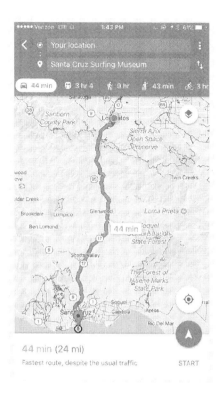

Press *Start* and Google Maps will talk you through getting from here to there. It calculates the fastest route given current and projected traffic patterns. If there's an accident, it reroutes you to the next best available route. You can look at how bad traffic is on any highway. If you want to compare routes, Google Maps will tell you how long each route will take. If you want to find the nearest coffee shop, it can tell you that too.

How does Google Maps accomplish all this deep magic? You guessed it, the cloud! Isn't the cloud cool?

To understand why the cloud is so important to Google

Maps, let's think about how it would need to work if Google Maps worked only on your device.

The first point to consider is that Google Maps works everywhere in the world for hundreds of millions of people. Keep in mind the storage available on any device is limited. How could Google Maps have the maps for everywhere in the world on your device? It couldn't. That's way too much data. All those maps are stored in the cloud (as data) and downloaded (over the internet) as needed.

The next point to consider is where does Google Maps get all the traffic information for every place in the world? Is there a way for your device to know all the traffic information, for everyplace in the world? No, there's not. That information must come from other sources.

In the US, for example, Google gets a lot of traffic information from Verizon. Verizon is a cellular network provider, so they can tell when people are stuck in traffic by tracking the location of all those cell phones. Google also gets traffic reports from local departments of transportation. And, since a lot of people use Google Maps, Google Maps tells Google about local traffic conditions too.

In short, Google gets traffic information from a lot of different sources. Those sources will be different depending on where you are. In India, traffic information is available from different sources than it is in Iowa. Google must make software systems to collect data from all those different sources. Is that possible on your device? No, it's not. It's way too big and complicated a problem for your little phone to handle.

After Google takes in all the traffic data, a picture must be generated of what traffic looks like at any given time, in any given place. Could this happen on your device? Not a chance. It requires a huge amount of data. Your phone couldn't handle it.

Now let's consider route planning. You may not know this, but planning a route is a genuinely difficult problem to solve. If you are at one point on the map, there are thousands of different roads you could take to get to a different point on the map. The best route is selected by predicting future travel times on each route and picking the one taking the least time. This requires a lot of information. Yes, it must know the current traffic conditions, but Google goes one step better. Google uses all the information they've collected over the years to predict likely traffic conditions, and they use their predictions when selecting a route. A lot of brainpower is needed to evaluate all those potential routes. Your phone can't do that.

The last thing we'll consider is Google Maps' ability to search for the nearest coffee shop. Google has to keep a giant points-of-interest map, so it knows about all the different things around you. Notice Google doesn't just show one coffee shop when you search for "best coffee shop." It gives you a list of shops and it also gives you a rating for each one, its hours of operation, how expensive it is, how far away you are from it now, and it will even show you a picture of what it looks like inside.

Here's an example of those search results:

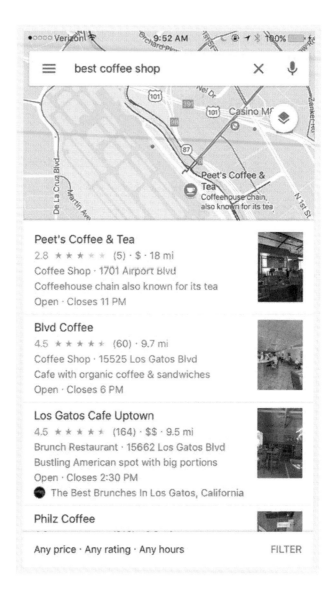

How does Google know all that? Because Google keeps that kind of data for literally every place in the world. No way that fits on your phone.

So far it seems like your phone is useless in the whole process. Everything of interest happens in the cloud. Not at all. Consider this. How does Google Maps know where you are at any one time? Your phone has a GPS feature (Global Positioning System). Using the GPS information from your phone, Google Maps continually reads your current location and sends it up to the cloud. The Google Maps app on your phone is responsible for showing you the route, telling you the turn-by-turn directions, and reacting to any commands you give. Google Maps will even store some data on your device so it can work for a little while without an internet connection.

Google Maps is **what a modern app looks like.** A lot happens in the cloud. You don't see it, but it's there, like an iceberg where 90% of the iceberg is underwater. Most of the heavy lifting is done in the cloud because the cloud has all the necessary resources to do the work.

But a lot happens on the phone too. If the internet connection goes down, Google Maps can't just stop working. That would be a disaster. An app needs enough data and enough smarts to do a lot of what the cloud does; only it must do it on the device. It's not easy to make that work.

There's a sophisticated dance of cooperation between a device and the cloud. It's quite beautiful when you think about it.

18

CLOUD DVR: TV IN THE CLOUD

Let's explain one final cloud service: the Cloud DVR. It's a good example of how a service can move from a local device to the cloud, and get a lot better in the process.

A DVR is a Digital Video Recorder. A DVR is a device connected to your TV that lets you record video to watch later. When you record a TV program, you're recording it on a DVR.

Here's a picture of our old DVR:

Yours probably looks similar. DVRs were an awesome invention. A DVR records a TV show so you can watch the show later, anytime you want. Such power! You don't need to be in front of a TV at a certain time anymore to watch a show. What an amazing freedom that is.

A DVR usually has a few standard features: it keeps a list of available shows for you to select from; it fast forwards past commercials (yeah!); it scrubs backward through video so a scene can be rewatched or be played in slow motion. A DVR may have lots of other features, but those are the basics.

A DVR usually has a few standard limitations as well: the number of simultaneous shows that can be recorded is limited by the number tuners, which means in practice only two shows can record at a time; the number of shows that can be stored on the DVR is limited. Once a DVR is full, old shows must be deleted to make room for new shows.

What do we know of that has unlimited space available? Oh yes, the cloud. So Cloud DVRs were invented.

YouTube TV, Sling TV, DirecTV Now, and Sony's Vue all are examples of services offering a Cloud DVR. A Cloud DVR is like the DVR that's attached to your TV, only it's in the cloud. You don't have a DVR box anymore. Instead, it's like any other cloud service we've described so far. You use an app to record and playback your shows.

Here's what YouTube TV looks like:

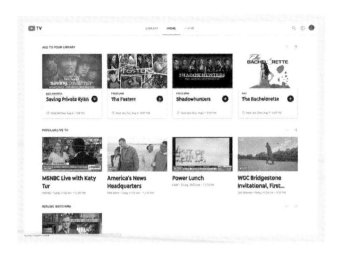

Searching for shows is like searching for anything else on Google. Select which shows you want to record and they'll record automatically.

And just like your old DVR, you can play a show back later, anytime you want, but there's a difference. YouTube TV lets you record six shows simultaneously, and there's no storage limit. You can store as much video as you want at no extra cost. And once you tell YouTube TV what your favorite show, league or team is, it will save all those games to your DVR, no matter on which channel they appear. Plus, you can watch those recordings on any device supporting YouTube TV, which is most everything.

Once again we see the benefits of moving to a cloud service.

The cloud service is smarter. The cloud has a massive amount of available resources. It learns what you like and automatically records shows it thinks you might want to watch later.

The cloud service has fewer limits. YouTube TV lets you record more video and keep more recordings.

The cloud service does more. YouTube TV can sort shows alphabetically, but you can also sort by *trending*, *top rated*, and *most popular*. Little features like this are easy to add to a cloud service.

The cloud service has a better user interface. DVR remotes and user interfaces are almost always slow, clunky, and difficult to use and understand.

The cloud service is easy to start using. Just sign up, and you can immediately start using YouTube TV.

The cloud service is easy to stop using. Tired of using YouTube TV? Cancel it. It's just that simple.

The cloud service doesn't have a physical device that needs replacing when it breaks. The cloud service provider is responsible for all maintenance.

On the negative side, if you don't have a good internet connection, a Cloud DVR won't work for you at all. The internet giveth and the internet taketh away.

19

WE'VE COME TO THE END OF OUR JOURNEY

I want to thank you for reading my book. I truly appreciate it!

If you don't mind, please review this book on amazon.com. It would help me attract more awesome readers like you.

Visit me online at Todd Hoff's Author Page on Facebook. We can chat there.

Want to be notified when I've published something new? Join Todd Hoff's newsletter on MailChimp.

You can also follow me on Todd Hoff's Author Page on Amazon.

And just another reminder, if you have any questions, please feel free to ask me anything on my Facebook group: <u>Tech for Mature Adults</u>. It would be my pleasure to help.

Printed in Great Britain
by Amazon